And Up They Flew

And Up They Flew

Martha Ross

And Up They Flew
first published 2009 by
Scirocco Drama
An imprint of J. Gordon Shillingford Publishing Inc.
© 2009 Martha Ross

Scirocco Drama Editor: Glenda MacFarlane
Cover design by Terry Gallagher / Dóowah Design Inc.
Author photo by John Launer
Printed and bound in Canada on 100% post-consumer recycled paper.

We acknowledge the financial support of the Manitoba Arts Council, The Canada Council for the Arts and the Government of Canada through the Book Publishing Industry Development Program (BPIDP) for our publishing program.

Production inquiries should be addressed to:
Martha Ross
129 Manning Avenue
Toronto, ON M6J 2K6

Library and Archives Canada Cataloguing in Publication

Ross, Martha, 1954-
    And up they flew / Martha Ross.

A play.
ISBN 978-1-897289-39-6

    I. Title.

PS8635.O6943 A65 2009   C812'.6   C2009-901364-9

J. Gordon Shillingford Publishing
P.O. Box 86, RPO Corydon Avenue, Winnipeg, MB Canada R3M 3S3

Special Thanks

In 2006, we produced a workshop production of *And Up They Flew*. I would like to extend a huge thank-you to the actors who were in this production: Tom Barnett, Paul Braunstein, Kate Hennig, Maggie Huculak, David Janssen, Tara Rosling and Jenny Young. Many thanks to the other actors who have been involved in various readings and contributed to the development of this play: Maev Beatty, Oliver Dennis, Sarah Dodd, Patrick Galligan, Tanja Jacobs, John Jarvis, Melody Johnson, Gray Powell, Rick Roberts, Julie Stewart and Waneta Storms. And I'd also like to extend a very hearty thank-you to the actors in the first production at Berkeley Street Theatre in Toronto in March, 2009—Paul Bernstein, John Cleland, Kerry Ann Doherty, Michelle Fisk, John Jarvis, Lisa Norton and Julie Stewart. They were extraordinary.

I would like to thank Emma Tibaldo of Playwrights' Workshop Montreal who not only provided countless hours of Dramaturgy, but also offered me invaluable support. And I'd like to thank Iris Turcott of CanStage, Alberta Theatre Projects and Vanessa Porteous.

I'd also like to extend a huge thank-you to Leah Cherniak, Jennifer Brewin, Deirdre Newman, Victoria Wallace, John Millard and Lily Ross-Millard for their unwavering support and patience, and a special expression of gratitude to my parents, Marion and Donald Ross, for their inspiration and their tireless dedication to the disarmament movement since the fifties.

Martha Ross

Martha Ross co-founded Theatre Columbus with Leah Cherniak in 1983, after she graduated from Ecole Jacques Lecoq in Paris. They have created thirty original comedies, including the internationally acclaimed *The Anger in Ernest and Ernestine* (1986); *The Attic, the Pearls and Three Fine Girls* (1995, 1998), for which Martha received a Dora Mavor Moore Award and was published by Scirocco Drama; and *The Betrayal*, which received a 1999 Chalmers Award for Best New Play. For other theatre companies Martha performed in a CanStage production of *The Overcoat*, and most recently, Les Saints' workshop production of Manon Beaudoin's tragicomedy *Queen of Hearts*.

As well as performing, Martha has written several plays, including *Porch People*; *Paranoia* (Dora Award); *Dr. Dapertutto* (nominated for the Chalmers Best New Play Award); *Ratbag*, a musical about the Industrial Revolution which she co-wrote with her husband, compser John Millard; *The Dog and the Angel* (1999); and *The Crack* (2002). She is currently writing a one-woman show, *On the Lam*, and *Home Town*, Pete Smith's Blyth Festival project.

Martha grew up outside of Vancouver and has lived in Toronto since the early eighties. She lives with her husband, John Millard, and their daughter, Lily Ross-Millard.

Characters

NORA Duckworth , the maid, Jane's childhood friend

JANE Ashbury, née McCleod, the hostess, Nora's childhood friend, Roger's wife

ROGER Ashbury, the host, Jane's husband

TED Pitt, a guest, Claire's husband

CLAIRE Pitt, a guest, Ted's wife

DAPHNE Crunchwell, Claire's 95-year-old cousin

MARLOW Stokes, a friend

Production Credits

And Up They Flew, a production of Theatre Columbus, premiered at the Berkeley Street Theatre Upstair, Toronto, on March 14, 2009, with the following cast:

NORA...Lisa Norton
JANE ....Kerry Ann Doherty
ROGER...John Cleland
TED...John Jarvis
CLAIRE...Julie Stewart
DAPHNE...Michelle Fisk
MARLOW...Paul Braunstein

Directed by Leah Cherniak
Set and Costume Design by Victoria Wallace
Lighting Design by Andrea Lundy
Sound Design by Lyon Smith
Video Design by Cameron Davis
Stage Manager: Tanya Greve

Playwright's Notes

Many years ago, twenty-five to be exact, Leah Cherniak and I founded our company, Theatre Columbus, with the mandate of creating physical theatre that has its own unique style: a comic style in which there is often the presence of a serious, sad, even tragic place. This is the kind of comedy that interests us. Comedy with weight. Comedy in which moments make you laugh, and then in an instant, make you cry. A comedy that has relevance to our time and place.

For many of our original creations, we begin with a theme. Themes about anger, paranoia, doubt, death, loneliness, and so on.

Before I wrote *And Up They Flew*, we began with an exploration period with some actors and the theme of *flight*. We improvised countless situations of packing, escaping and fleeing. We delved into our dreams of flying and imitated many a bird. It didn't take long before we discovered that the places we were going to were sometimes joyous, sometimes melancholic, sometimes anxious, sometimes profoundly sad. And we explored gravity, and those moments when you can't leave a room or situation.

At some point it was decided that I would write a play, using our exploration of flight as imspiration. The physical energy of fleeing led me to writing a farce-like comedy. It became apparent to me that I wanted to set this comedy between the wars, a time in history that I have always been interested in, as it tells us so much about the advent of our current tensions, globally and individually.

I would like to extend a huge thank you to all of the actors who worked with us throughout the process. Again and again they fueled my imagination and my vision of this play's world of play. The true essence of theatre, I believe, is exactly that: it's about the actor and the spirit of the play.

The comic style that is inherent to this play is a tricky one to describe. The actors have to be true and at the same time, 'larger than life'. The characters are all caught in their various emotional quagmaires of denial, self-deception, and paralysis. They are all struggling with their own predicaments of being trapped—by their marriages, by their work, their sense of failure, their memories of the World War I, and by the looming inevitability of the next war. The on-going search when approaching *And Up They Flew* is to find the lightness in the gravity, and the gravity in the lightness.

It is perhaps worth noting that for our first production in Toronto, we utilized a video design by Cameron Davis, in order to show Nora's dream and also the dreams experienced by Nora and Marlow in the 'dream machine'.

Act I

The year is 1919 in the northeast of England. NORA and JANE, two friends, eleven and thirteen years old, sit on a little bluff or possibly a structure that suggests a tree. They are waiting to catch sight of the first, nonstop transatlantic flight made by the pilots Alcock and Brown, from Newfoundland to Ireland.

NORA: I'm ecstatic the war is o'er and all, Janey, but why does it still feel like shite?

JANE: *(Impatient sigh.)* I don't know Nora. Just bloody watch the sky.

NORA amuses herself by quacking like a duck. JANE controls her temper and sighs menacingly.

NORA: Are you sure we're in the reet part of England Jane?

JANE: *(Hides her uncertainty.)* Yes, I'm sure. The sky's not that bloody big.

NORA quacks.

Shh!

NORA groans.

Shh!

NORA: Janey.

JANE: Nora! You haven't bloody shut yer gob since we snuck out. How'll we catch sight of the first flight o'er the Atlantic with you gan on an on, it's the first flight o'er the Atlantic Nora!

NORA: It's just I haven't had a crumb to eat all day.

JANE: *(Exasperated but sympathetic sigh.)* Yer stepfather's bloody evil to not feed you just cause you talk too much. You poor thing. *(Gives her a biscuit from her pocket.)*

NORA: Thanks awfully Jane. Me poor Mum before she died said Mr. Tim gets evil on account of the mud in his brain, you know, from the trenches.

JANE: No offence to yer poor dead Mum Nora, but that doesn't make a scrap of sense. Yer stepfather's just plain evil, that's all there's to it.

NORA: I know what I'm gan to do, Jane. I'm gan to pick up me wings and fly out of this shite hole.

JANE: Are you now?

NORA: I'll lift me arms an then a puff-a-wind'll take me up to the sky and then Mr. Tim will gandie up and say, "What's got into Nora now, she's like flying with the swallows!" To which I'll reply, "Goodbye forever, Mr. Tim! Not so nice knowing you! So bugger off!" *(Laughs.)*

JANE: *(Laughs.)* Nora Duckworth!

NORA: Won't that be grand Jane, to just up and fly away from it all?

JANE: *(Stops laughing.)* But Nora, you know you cannit just pick up yer arms an fly. You do know that. Don't you?

NORA: But I dream about it all the time Jane. I fly up with the swallows, just me and the swallows.

JANE: But that's just a dream!

NORA: I know it's a dream Janey, cause I dream it, doesn't mean I cannit do it.

JANE: Yes it does mean you cannit do it! Yer reet daft! Now be quiet or we'll miss seeing the pilots! Crikey! Don't worry Nora, lucky for you, I'm gan to marry a rich man and I'll have him buy two aeroplanes, one for you an one for me, an it'll be canny grand, you'll see, Nora, it'll all be fine.

NORA: I don't want an aeroplane.

JANE: *(Raises her hand.)* I, Janey McCleod, yer beloved friend and neighbour from birth, do solemnly swear to take care of you, Nora Duckworth, forever an ever. *(Spits.)*

NORA: Forever an ever?

JANE: Mud in his brain from the trenches. *(Bursts into laughter.)* "Bugger off!"

           NORA laughs with JANE. They improvise a few lines about telling Mr. Tim and others to "bugger off!" We see just how much they love each other. NORA loses her balance and falls. JANE screams.

           Nora!

NORA: It's all reet Jane. I landed in a bush! Ow.

           They laugh. Music.

           The music continues, the set becomes the living room of the Ashbury's country home. The year is now 1936. ROGER Ashbury and his guests CLAIRE and TED Pitt, and MARLOW Stokes, dance after dinner. JANE, who is now married to ROGER, joins them. TED, who is somewhat drunk, keeps tripping over CLAIRE. CLAIRE and ROGER make eyes at each other throughout.

TED: Sorry darling. I seem to have acquired a third left foot.

They all sit.

CLAIRE: Really dear? I hadn't noticed. Ooh la la! I ate too much duck.

ROGER: The duck was very tasty tonight, we must compliment the cook. Will you remind me Jane? I forget that sort of thing.

JANE: Yes Roger, you do forget that sort of thing.

TED: Ah yes, "lest we forget".

CLAIRE: Please Teddy, not another war story. You went on and on at dinner.

ROGER: I don't always forget that sort of thing.

JANE: Some people like to compliment, others don't, that's all.

            NORA, now a maid, makes a comic entrance with a drink trolley. She bumps into ROGER.

ROGER: Ow!

NORA: Sorry!

            ROGER glares menacingly at NORA. NORA feeds their caged bird.

CLAIRE: After all, the war's been over for about a million years.

ROGER: Eighteen, Claire, actually.

TED: There's going to be another one, it's in the air, you can smell it.

ROGER: I personally don't smell a thing.

NORA: *(To the bird.)* Coo, coo. *(Takes a book from her pocket and reads.)*

CLAIRE: You have to keep your nostrils open, Roger,

it's an Eastern concept, I know this exercise. *(Demonstrates.)*

ROGER: I'm sure you do a splendid exercise, Claire, I'm just saying that we don't know there'll be another war. It's safe to say we don't know much of anything. *(Waves his arms at NORA to start serving drinks. JANE notices.)*

JANE: *(Under her breath.)* Nora! *(Attempts through gesture to tell NORA to put her book away and serve drinks and that ROGER is quite fed up, etc.)*

> DAPHNE Crunchwell, CLAIRE's elderly cousin, enters. She's looking for something.

CLAIRE: Daphne. Daphne dear! She never sits anymore. *(Short, loud laugh.)*

TED: They're gearing up as we sit here like insane white lumps. Has anyone noticed how we seem to be getting whiter and lumpier by the second?

> DAPHNE exits.

CLAIRE: Daphne? Oh, dear. It would be amusing if it weren't so sad. *(Short, loud laugh.)*

> NORA crosses In front of MARLOW.

MARLOW: I have always been fascinated by how the neck hangs.

JANE: How what neck hangs, Marlow?

MARLOW: The neck of a dead duck of course.

JANE: Really? I hadn't noticed how the neck of a dead duck hangs.

ROGER: Don't encourage him dear. She always does you know.

JANE: No I don't Roger.

ROGER: Yes you do dear, but it's no big thing, just funny.
            That's all.

JANE: It wasn't me who invited him this weekend!

ROGER: I said it's no big thing!

MARLOW: *(Raises his glass.)* Here's to the weekend. *(Looks at
            JANE.)* Here's to old friends.

            DAPHNE enters, still looking for something.

CLAIRE: Daphne! Come join us!

DAPHNE: Have you seen my cushion Clarabelle? It's just up
            and vanished.

CLAIRE: Dear me, she has this special cushion.

DAPHNE: *(To NORA.)* Don't lose things my dear. When you
            have something don't lose it. But who are you?

CLAIRE: She's the maid, Daphne!

DAPHNE: I know a maid when I see one. She's not a maid.

JANE: Lady Crunchwell, do you need any assistance?
            Perhaps the maid could be of some assistance.
            (Throws NORA a look.)

NORA: Yes, um could I be of any assistance, Lady
            Spongewell?

JANE: *(Under her breath.)* Crunchwell Nora, it's
            Crunchwell.

DAPHNE: If you could help me find my head. *(Exits.)*

ROGER: Your cousin, Claire, should join Scotland Yard.
            (Imitates her.)

            *CLAIRE laughs too long. NORA serves MARLOW
            a drink.*

MARLOW: One day, Jane, you'll have to come duck hunting

with me. It brings us face to face with our primordial self. It's profoundly sexual.

CLAIRE: Profoundly sexual. Really Marlow.

JANE: Yes. Really Marlow.

MARLOW: *(To NORA.)* What a beautiful brooch. Where did you get such an exquisite piece?

NORA: Uh…a friend gave it to me.

MARLOW: A golden swallow. *(Rubs the brooch.)* Beautiful.

NORA: *(Spills a few drops on MARLOW.)* Sorry!

MARLOW: Quite alright.

ROGER: Perhaps we need more music. *(Puts on a record.)*

JANE: But I want to hear from Marlow how our primordial, sexual self looks like a dead duck.

> ROGER gestures to JANE that NORA is making him crazy. She gestures back.

MARLOW: My theory Jane, is that if we truly look into the eyes of death, only then can we know who we are.

TED: "Who we are"? We're idiots. "War to end all wars." What a load of unmitigated crap.

CLAIRE: Oh Ted! Jane I wish you hadn't brought up the subject of that ghastly battle whatever it was…

ROGER: Passion –dale, I believe it was Claire. Passion dale. *(Slyly winks at her and dances by himself.)*

CLAIRE: Yes Roger, that's what it was. *(Makes secret eyes at him.)* Jane? Are you alright dear?

JANE: Hmm? Oh! No. I'm fine. Yes, I'm fine.

ROGER: She's thinking about her damn plane. I never should have bought the damn thing. Now she's talking about being the first woman to fly the Atlantic.

CLAIRE: Jane!

JANE: *(Makes a slow cross to the grmophone and stops the music.)* Earhart has already flown the Atlantic, Roger, but no woman has flown East to West. Solo.

ROGER: Why I asked all of you here this weekend. Thought you could talk her out of it.

CLAIRE: Really Roger, is that why you asked us here?

ROGER: Something like that. *(Throws CLAIRE a sly wink.)*

MARLOW: Are you really going to do it Jane?

JANE: Well it would be wonderful to win the title. My mechanic thinks I should do it, that sort of thing. It would be awfully exciting. And the wind will be right in a week. *(Knocks on wood.)*

MARLOW: Why anyone would want to go flying in the bloody freezing sky, just to win some little title, is beyond me. *(Knocks on wood.)*

CLAIRE: Her mechanic thinks she should do it.

MARLOW: Oh, her mechanic, well then!

CLAIRE: We would miss you terribly Jane.

JANE: It's just a thought, nothing too serious, just a whim.

TED: Take me with you Janey McCleod, I'm tired of importing tea. I'm tired of being English! Fly me anywhere! Fly me to Tahiti!

JANE: I'm sorry Ted, it has to be solo.

MARLOW: I once went to Tahiti with a beautiful Egyptian woman, but I was on a good old boat.

JANE: Perhaps you and your fiancée should take a boat

trip after you get married, which is soon, isn't it Marlow?

CLAIRE: Marlow getting married! I keep forgetting.

JANE: Yes, Marlow, when do we get to meet this new fiancée of yours?

MARLOW: I like shy women, you know that Jane.

JANE: Well, we're beginning to think she doesn't exist! (*Laughs.*)

> *MARLOW glowers at her. DAPHNE enters.*

CLAIRE: Daphne! Do sit down!

DAPHNE: Damn. Back where I started from. (*Exits.*)

> *TED falls off his chair.*

CLAIRE: I think we should call it an evening. (*Looks at ROGER.*)

ROGER: (*Yawns.*) Yes, perhaps we should.

JANE: (*Yawns.*) We have all weekend, after all.

MARLOW: I'm looking forward to it. (*Turns to NORA; NORA spills some drink on his lap.*)

ROGER: That's the last straw. Bloody, bloody hell. Why are you always spilling things on my guests. I won't have it.

JANE: She's not always spilling things on our guests.

ROGER: Just last night she spilled gravy on my new trousers.

MARLOW: I really don't mind.

JANE: Your new trousers can't really be called guests.

> *TED walks, unnoticed, into a closet.*
>
> *DAPHNE enters.*

CLAIRE: Daphne! We're going to bed now!

DAPHNE: I can't find anything in this house, the rooms make no sense.

MARLOW: I really don't mind.

CLAIRE: We should all go to bed.

JANE: She just needs some more time to get used to things.

ROGER: How much time does a maid need Jane, how much time?

CLAIRE: Ted, I'm going to bed. Where is he? Well I'm sure I'll manage by myself. *(Exits while looking at ROGER meaningfully.)*

ROGER: Yes. It certainly is time for bed. *(To NORA.)* We'll talk about your employ at another time. *(He trips over sofa and falls into it. Exits.)*

MARLOW: Good sleep to all. I'll be off. *(To NORA.)* To my room. On the right. *(Exits.)*

DAPHNE: But where is everyone going?

JANE/
NORA: To bed!

DAPHNE: Well good luck is what I say. Going to bed is the most difficult thing, sometimes it can take all day. *(Exits.)*

NORA: *(Watching DAPHNE.)* Isn't she fascinating. *(Turns.)* Jane. Are you really going to fly o'er the Atlantic?

JANE: What? Yes. I don't know. But Nora! You have to be better at being a maid. Roger will get suspicious that we're friends.

NORA: And remind me why Roger shouldn't know that we're friends.

JANE: Nora, Roger is Roger and Roger is... limited. He wouldn't understand why I had to hire you because we're old friends. He doesn't understand things like friendship or childhood or being an adult, or really much of anything.

NORA: Why did you marry him then?

JANE: Oh you know.

NORA: No.

JANE: Oh I don't know!

NORA: You canny lied to Roger about where you grew up, dinnit you?

JANE Well of course I did. Aargh! And this bird is getting fat! Who ever heard of a fat bird! He looks depressed! Oh my head is bursting. (Sits.)

NORA: (To the bird.) Poor little thing. You're not so fat.

JANE: I have so much to do to get my plane ready.

> NORA attempts to cheer up the bird by making funny duck sounds, etc.

NORA: Did you know there are people in India who travel in their heads while sitting on their beds? Wouldn't that be handy, Jane? We wouldn't have to go anywhere, or fly anywhere for that matter.

JANE: (Groans.) Oh, my head.

NORA: How about I make you some of my blackberry tea? Blackberry leaves are a cure for all kinds of ailments.

JANE: I'm just going to go to bed. Good night Nora. (Exits.)

NORA: G'night.

JANE: *(Enters.)* Do you remember when we went looking for those pilots and you fell into those blackberry bushes. And then Mr. Tim found us and you told him we'd been stolen by a silver light in the sky?

                > *They explode with laughter. They laugh briefly and too loudly. They stop laughing and stare at each other awkwardly. JANE exits.*

                > *NORA stares into space, remembering.*

                (Enters.) Oh! And Nora! I don't think it's proper to receive gifts from guests. *(Nervously indicates a "brooch".)* It's a bit...you know... *(Beat. She exits and bumps into MARLOW.)* Marlow! What are you doing prowling about like a wolf in the woods? As if I didn't know.

MARLOW: Just looking for a pleasant nightcap, that's all Jane.

JANE: Then perhaps you need the maid.

MARLOW: Good idea. The maid.

JANE: Watch it, Marlow! *(Beat. Exits.)*

MARLOW: What ever could she mean, "Watch it Marlow!"?

                > *MARLOW fixes himself a drink. NORA turns away and takes off her brooch in order to examine it.*

                You have one of the most beautiful cold shoulders.

NORA: *(Faces him.)* Why did you ask who gave me the brooch. I don't know why you gave me the brooch and I don't know why you asked who gave me the brooch, when you know who gave me the brooch.

MARLOW: It's quite simple.

NORA: It is?

MARLOW: *(Moving closer.)* Quite simply, Nora, I wanted to see you blush. I love how the nape of your neck quivers when you blush.

NORA: It does? *(Attempts to look at her neck.)*

MARLOW: You're like some kind of creature, sipping water at the edge of the jungle. Alert and waiting. What are you waiting for, I wonder? *(MARLOW touches NORA's breast and she faints with a thud. She drops the brooch.)* Damn. Nora! Damn! Why does this always happen to me? *(Waves things to revive her while calling out the door.)* Someone! Someone! Blast it. Bloody damn blast it. Jane!

JANE: *(Enters.)* Feeling a bit helpless are we Marlow?

MARLOW: Would you get off your high cloud and notice that Nora, the maid, your childhood friend, a fact that for some reason is a big secret from big Roger, has fainted.

JANE: And who could have caused this bizarre occurrence? *(Kneels by NORA and fans her.)*

MARLOW: Can I help it if I make women hyperventilate. Surely you haven't forgotten?

JANE: My name's not Shirley. *(Goes to get smelling salts.)* But perhaps you're confusing me with your fiancée before me, or perhaps the one after?

MARLOW: You exaggerate and as usual show no compassion.

JANE: Poor Marlow for drowning in his father's inheritance. But wouldn't your father have been pleased at how well you do nothing. *(Saunters back to NORA.)* Oh except when you're pretending to be an inventor of gadgets that never work.

MARLOW: Sometimes they're successful.

JANE: Name one! *(Kneels down beside MARLOW.)*

MARLOW: Ever heard of going quickly during a medical emergency?

JANE: Have you ever heard of moving over? *(Pushes MARLOW out of the way.)*

MARLOW: *(Pushes JANE.)* You move over!

JANE: She's my friend!

MARLOW: Really, you don't say!

JANE: It's not me who's about to break her heart. Giving her your mother's brooch!

MARLOW: Let it go Mrs. Ashbury!

JANE: Let what go pray tell?!

MARLOW: The fact that I broke your heart a million years ago, a poor country girl, lost in London, you should be over it by now.

JANE: If I remember correctly it was me who broke your heart.

MARLOW: If you'll recall dear lady, it was me, who left you.

JANE: You left me because you knew that I was going to leave you. You knew that I knew that the whole thing was silly.

MARLOW: Who is silly? Flying across the Atlantic. You call that not silly?!

JANE: I'm a damn good pilot Marlow!

MARLOW: Tell that to the cow you crashed into.

NORA: *(Coming to.)* He came back.

JANE: Nora! Who came back ?

NORA: The old Haida Chief, from Canada.

JANE: Oh no, not him again.

NORA: He tried to lift me, just like tha last time, but couldn't, and then a raven came along and it tried, and it couldn't. I was completely stuck on the ground and couldn't fly. It was the oddest thing.

JANE: Nora. It was just a dream.

NORA: I know that Jane.

MARLOW: She knows that Jane.

JANE: Alright!

DAPHNE enters.

DAPHNE: I'll pretend to be sorry for interrupting youth but I must find my cushion, is there a maid or some such person, ah there you are, lying down I see, well good for you.

NORA: *(Feeling nervous with MARLOW.)* I'd better help Mrs. Crunchwell's cushion find her cousin. I mean Mrs. Cushion find her crunch. Excuse me. *(Exits.)*

JANE: Leave her alone, Marlow. Now go to bed. Your own bed. *(Storms out.)*

MARLOW: *(To DAPHNE.)* After all these years, she's the only woman who can truly make my blood boil. *(He exits.)*

DAPHNE: *(Hasn't heard a word.)* Strange. That man made me feel faint.

CLAIRE and ROGER enter, from opposite sides.

CLAIRE: Daphne! Go to bed!

DAPHNE: Easy for you to say. Being almost a century old is unnavigible. But where could I have put it? Damn and bloody damn. *(Slow exit.)*

They feed the bird and wait until she is gone. ROGER pounces on CLAIRE. Comic embracing.

CLAIRE: Roger!

ROGER: Oh Claire, you peach, you divine peach, we're
             alone, I couldn't wait one more second and not
             squeeze your divine peach-ness.

CLAIRE: Oh Roger, I can't bear my husband any longer, his
             sadness is killing me; he lives in a grave.

ROGER: I can't bear my wife, when I'm with her I'm thinking
             of you and when I'm with you I'm thinking of you
             and when I'm with her she's thinking of flying, I'm
             so sick of flying this, flying that, it's aggravating
             but when I'm with you I think of nothing but your
             peach-ness, your, peachy- peaches.

CLAIRE: (Swoons.) Oh Roger.

ROGER: I love it when you call me…Roger. Do it again.

CLAIRE: Roger.

ROGER: Oh, again!

CLAIRE: Roger.

ROGER: You're turning me into a desperate stallion.

                 CLAIRE runs away and squeals.

             I'm a strutting peacock. (Demonstrates. CLAIRE
             squeals.) No! I'm a hot and bothered bull! You make
             me into a bull.

                 They engage in a game of bull and matador — miming
                 a cape, much giggling, snorting, etc.

CLAIRE: Oh! At last we're alone

                 JANE enters, sees what's going on. Hides behind a
                 plant.

ROGER: Oh, at last, at last, (Tries unsuccessfully to undo her
             dress.)

CLAIRE: But I feel so guilty, we're so guilty.

ROGER: We're not guilty yet, madam, we have yet to...we have yet to...how do I get these, oh I want to feel your naked, where are you?

CLAIRE: Oh Roger. I hope you don't mind! I brought my cousin Daphne. She seemed so dreadfully out of sorts.

ROGER: Yes, yes, very nice, aren't we all. Oh Peach! You make me insane with desire, these buttons are making me insane, they won't, I can't, I might have to rip you open , stand still Claire!!

CLAIRE thinks she hears a noise.

CLAIRE: Roger! What was that?

ROGER: It's a plot from God to test us. But to hell with God! *(Lunges at her, they fall to the floor and writhe around.)*

CLAIRE: *(Sits up.)* What if it's Ted? What if it's Jane?!

ROGER: I don't hear anyone! *(Lunges at her.)*

CLAIRE: Roger! We have to control ourselves! *(CLAIRE runs off.)*

ROGER: I'm tired of controlling myself! I don't want to control myself anymore! Claire! *(Runs after her and steps on NORA's brooch. Screams. Throws brooch. Exits.)*

JANE comes out of her hiding place, just as TED falls out of the closet, with a bucket on his foot.

JANE: *(Startled.)* Ted! Where did you...what did you... *(Not knowing what he's heard.)* You should go to bed, Ted.

TED: No, no. Beds are scary places. The loneliness is more deafening than a battlefield.

JANE: Yes. I know what you mean. I mean, I don't. But I do.

TED: Are you really going to fly across the Atlantic Jane?

JANE: *(Stunned.)* The wind will be right in a week. But I have to think about Roger. No I don't! But then there's Nora, the maid, and of course the strong possibility of a storm, over the ocean, and I can't swim, I'll have to decide soon, that's all, I don't know. *(Holds back tears.)*

TED: You're in shock, Jane. It will most likely pass. Goodnight my dear. *(Exits.)*

JANE: Goodnight, Ted.

                ROGER enters, sees JANE and runs out, hoping she didn't see him. CLAIRE enters from another entrance, sees JANE and exits. DAPHNE enters.

DAPHNE: Ah, Mrs. Whatever your name is. Perhaps you could help me, it's only of the utmost importance.

JANE: Hello Lady Crunchwell. You might as well be the first to know. I'm going to fly across the Atlantic! A week from today. The wind is definitely right. *(Exits.)*

DAPHNE: Wind?! That's all I need, to be blown over then how would I get back up, that's a laugh but not really.

                NORA enters. She's looking for her brooch.

                Ah. It's the maid who isn't a maid. Tell me, do you feel, "caught"?

NORA: Caught? *(Confused.)* No.

DAPHNE: *(Takes out a tin.)* Humbug?

NORA: No thank you.

DAPHNE: Can't put my finger on it. *(Starts to exit.)*

NORA: *(To herself.)* Caught? *(To DAPHNE.)* Lady Crunchwell, have you seen Marlow? I mean, Mr. Stokes? But actually I'm looking for my brooch.

DAPHNE: What you're really looking for my dear is your head. That Archduke what's his name, Ferdinand in Austria was shot and then we all lost our heads, we all went a bit mad, everything is completely ruined now. We carved up all the countries, now we'll get carved. No telling what will happen. Nothing to do but toss and turn in our little beds and worry ourselves sick. *(Starts to exit.)* We'll be lucky if we ever sleep again.

NORA: Oh! Lady Crunchwell. I found your cushion! *(Gives it to her.)*

DAPHNE: My cushion.! Oh. I'm saved. How can I thank you. My cushion. *(Emotion. Exits.)*

        NORA puts on a record and dances comically. MARLOW sneaks up on her.

NORA: *(Screams.)* Ahhh! *(Removes music.)* Where did you come from?

MARLOW: From thin air. Poof.

NORA: Poof?

MARLOW: I've been lying in bed thinking about you Nora.

NORA: Really?

MARLOW: I've been building a little something and I've decided to give it to you. Shhh. Someone's coming. It could be Jane. She seems to be following me. *(Hides behind sofa.)*

        TED crosses, still with the bucket on his foot. MARLOW tries unsuccessfully to remove it. Exits.

MARLOW: Damn. Shh. Someone's coming again. It could be Jane. *(Hides behind sofa.)*

        JANE enters.

JANE: Nora.

NORA: Jane.

JANE: I can't sleep Nora. I need to talk.

NORA: I can't really talk at the moment Jane. I...have some
               late dusting to do.

JANE: Really?!

NORA: I'll come find you later with some of my blackberry
               tea.

JANE: *(Sighs.)* Please hurry! *(Exits. MARLOW pops up.*
               JANE re-enters, MARLOW pops down.) Watch out for
               Marlow, Nora. He's to be avoided. *(Exits.)*

               MARLOW pops up. JANE enters, MARLOW pops
               down.

               Are you sure that's the proper way to dust? Oh
               never mind. *(Exits.)*

MARLOW: You have to talk her out of it Nora!

NORA: Sorry?

MARLOW: Hmm?

NORA: What were you saying Marlow?

MARLOW: Oh yes. What was I saying. Before Jane intercepted
               us like some goddamn referee! Oh yes. Just that I
               like to tinker with inventions. I'm somewhat of a
               tinkerer , a fiddler if you like, I like to fiddle, I like
               to dream, fiddle, dream, fiddle, dream, I guess we
               all like to do that.

NORA: I love dreaming.

MARLOW: Well that's why I'm giving you my "dream
               machine", Nora.

NORA: A dream machine?!

MARLOW: I've been working on it for years, it's not quite finished , but when it is we could hook up to it, no interruptions, no Jane, being nosy, sticking her nose in where she shouldn't.

NORA: She does that doesn't she? What I mean is, we are adults after all.

MARLOW: Yes, we are. *(Heavy breathing.)* I have this dream Nora that you slowly bend over me, and you ask if I want more gravy, and I say, yes, more gravy, and then I reach under the table and I slowly lift your skirt and oh my, what's that, it's your hot quivering thighs, they're all...quivery, and then, I move over to your sweating buttocks, and up to your hard waiting breasts, then you roll me onto the floor, we meet like beasts in the jungle, we're drenched in steamy, hot expectation, there's an arched back, a leap and we tear into each other like *(NORA faints.)* Oh bloody damn, not again! *(Revives NORA as before.)*

          JANE enters looking for NORA.

JANE: Marlow!

MARLOW: Surprise, surprise! It's Jane! The pilot. Or is it the ground crew? Can't sleep Jane? Seems like none of us can. *(NORA comes to.)* Why hello Nora. If you need anything, you know where to find me. In my bed. Not sleeping. Waiting. For gravy. Goodnight Jane! *(Exits.)*

JANE: Nora! What are you doing!? He's about to be married you know.

NORA: I can quite manage by myself, Jane.

JANE: Well I don't know how you'll manage if Roger fires you while I'm gone.

NORA: You're going to do it then!

JANE: Yes Nora, I'm going to do it. I'm going to fly across the Atlantic. Yes, I am! I didn't know how serious I was until I found Roger, wrapped around, *(Sniffs.)* Claire.

NORA: Yes, yes, yes, but Jane, the Atlantic, it's so gigantic.

JANE: *(Stunned.)* What do you mean "yes, yes, yes"?

NORA: All those waves, heaving and swelling, dark and foreboding, you know, below you.

JANE: Did you know about Roger and Claire?

NORA: Cold, merciless abyss. *(Imitates sounds of ocean.)*

JANE: You did know about Roger and Claire!

NORA: Well I'm not blind, am I now?

JANE: I can't believe that you knew and you didn't... Claire was my bridesmaid!

NORA: But Jane, I thought you knew.

JANE: You thought I knew?! How would I know!

NORA: Because it's so obvious and I didn't think you cared!

JANE: I'm just going to go to bed. I'm just going to go to bed and then I'll fly o'er the Atlantic. *(Starts to exit.)*

NORA: You're running away Jane! You always run away!

JANE: Me! Who's always moving here, moving there? You never stop moving!

NORA: We were talking about you Jane.

JANE: Who in this room has never had one relationship in her life?!

NORA: I relate to the people in the village!

JANE: *(Sarcastic.)* "The people in the village."

NORA: What has happened to you Jane?

JANE: More like what has not happened to you Nora!

NORA: Sorry?!

JANE: How many times have I found you without a penny to your name? Last time I found you in a cow barn nestled in a mound of moldy old books!

NORA: I like reading!

JANE: Face facts Nora! You wouldn't have a hope in hell of surviving without me.

NORA: Perhaps you should face facts Jane. After the guests leave, I'm quitting.

JANE: You're quitting?

NORA: Yes Jane. I quit. Forever and ever. Do you understand?

           CLAIRE runs upstage, chased by ROGER.

JANE: Very well then. Good then. Good night then. *(Starts to exit.)*

NORA: Jane!

JANE: What?!

NORA: Why wasn't I your bridesmaid?

JANE: Isn't it obvious? *(Emotional exit. She gets tangled in curtains.)*

           Sad beat. NORA looks at the bird. Lies down on the sofa and goes to sleep. Music. DAPHNE enters and takes an envelope out of her cushion, opens it for the first time and reads the letter. Emotional beat. She hides the letter in the cushion. Exits. Sounds of wings flapping. The sound intensifies. NORA has a disturbing dream that includes her, the Haida chief, JANE, and an aborted flight. She wakes up and exits.

> *Transition. The characters wander in and out. A sleepless night.*
>
> *Next day. Early afternoon. CLAIRE and DAPHNE enter the living room.*

CLAIRE: I feel so confined. Don't you feel confined?

DAPHNE: Why on earth do you feel fine?

CLAIRE: I'm not fine Cousin Daphne! I asked you if you feel confined?!

DAPHNE: Of course I feel confined, I'm confined in my own saggy skin.

CLAIRE: *(In her own thoughts.)* You don't sag at all Daphne.

DAPHNE: *(Offers her a candy.)* Humbug?

> *CLAIRE declines. DAPHNE steals this moment to take out her letter from her cushion and read it.*

CLAIRE: Have you seen Mr. Ashbury today?

DAPHNE: Who's getting buried today? *(Hides her letter.)*

CLAIRE: No, not buried, Roger.

DAPHNE: What are you talking about Clarabelle?

CLAIRE: Nothing. I got no sleep last night. Running here, running there. *(Softly.)* It's so difficult having an affair.

DAPHNE: Who's having an affair?

CLAIRE: What?! What are you talking about Daphne? *(Fans herself.)* Daphne, Ted and I are going through a difficult... Roger... says hello. *(Beat.)* There's no air in here! *(Rings bell.)*

DAPHNE: Well, I won't send him a photo of myself, no, I won't do that.

CLAIRE: Hmm?

DAPHNE: Nothing!

> *NORA enters reading a book, while wheeling in a tea trolley that is not co-operating. She bumps into furniture as she zigzags across the room. DAPHNE sneaks another look at her letter.*

CLAIRE: Maid, please open the window. I can't breathe.

NORA: Oh my. Yes mam. Right away, mam.

> *NORA finds the long window stick. Comic business as she keeps almost hitting CLAIRE and DAPHNE.*
>
> *She stands on a step unit and attempts to open a window. There's a sound of JANE's airplane overhead.*

CLAIRE: That must be Jane, in her plane. Oh Jane. What to do, what to do?

DAPHNE: If God, not that He exists, had wanted us to fly, He would have made us with little wings sprouting from our shoulder bones, what are they called, wing bones.

CLAIRE: You have to expand how you imagine God, Daphne, maybe even imagine him as a her.

DAPHNE: *(Looks at her cushion.)* You sound like Rupert.

CLAIRE: Who dear?

DAPHNE: Rupert.

CLAIRE: Who's Rupert?

DAPHNE: I don't know.

NORA: *(Gasps.)* I dreamt about that old chief again!

CLAIRE: What is your name cherie?

NORA: *(Sits down to have tea with them.)* It's Nora Duckworth mam, although some call me Nora

Plonk, but I loath that name, seeing as it was my stepfather's name who is quite dead but when he was alive, he was a veritable monster. Had one glass eye, a wooden leg, and when he talked, which was seldom, he growled, like this *(Demonstrates.)*. Oh he was bad as they come. I strongly suspect he had somewhat of a hand in the sudden death of me poor mother. Rolled over in the middle of the night and speared her with the metal that was in his body from the war. Jane, Mrs. Ashbury, never believed me, but that shouldn't surprise you, she's somewhat limited. Me poor dear mother. I miss her something fierce.

CLAIRE: I too miss my mother. Sometimes I think it's all too much. *(Bursts into tears. Comic, but sad.)*

            NORA gets up and trips. The lights flicker.

CLAIRE: *(Gasps.)* Wasn't that odd how upon the mention of your poor mother's suspicious death, you tripped. For no apparent reason. And then the lights flickered. *(Smiles slyly.)*

DAPHNE: Clarabelle. You're not?!

CLAIRE: Yes, I most certainly am.

DAPHNE: You're not!

CLAIRE: Yes, Daphne! A séance! But the men must not know about it. Men make the spirits shy.

            TED enters, exits, enters, exits, distraught and oblivious. He crashes into something offstage.

DAPHNE: What has got into your husband Claire?

CLAIRE: It's the war. It's always the war, oh I don't know. It could be gas.

NORA: I have an ancient cure for gas. I'll see if I can be of assistance. *(Exits.)*

DAPHNE: I do like that girl, but something is holding her hostage.

CLAIRE: *(In her own thoughts.)* Hmmm.

DAPHNE: Claire. A few days ago I received a very important love letter.

CLAIRE: A séance. Yes. Oh Maman! *(Wipes away a tear.)*

> *Lights shift to TED and CLAIRE's small room. TED is packing. NORA knocks on the door.*

TED: I'm not here.

> *NORA knocks again.*

(Opens the door.) I'm not here!

NORA: I'm sorry for bothering you, Mr. Pitt, when you're not here, but your wife tells me that you have a bad case of gas.

TED: Does my wife say that? She's so very considerate, that wife of mine.

NORA: The only thing that my evil stepfather taught me was how to correct a bad case of gas. This is what you do, if you please sir. *(Comical demonstration.)*

TED: *(Chuckles, then starts to cry. He stops himself.)* My mother used to tell me this story about a little boy who couldn't stay on the ground, so his parents put him in lead boots to keep him from floating away. *(Emotional beat. Tries to close suitcase. NORA tries to help. Stops.)* I was standing in the mud with my best chum, Burt. He was from Canada. A wonderful fellow. Suddenly, shells start to explode, and this big chap, forget his name, he gets hit and falls on me, and I can't move, I'm completely pinned down. Burt tries to help but he keeps slipping in the mud and we start to laugh, we laugh so hard it hurts. And then out of nowhere, Burt gets hit. He blows way up into the air, and his arms and legs fall down on me, like little gifts from the sky. Then his head, looking impossibly like his head, lands in the mud, this far away. I remember thinking, *(Emotion.)* Burt should have put on his boots. He should have put on his lead boots and stayed at home. *(Weeps.)*

NORA: *(Handing him a tissue.)* What a sad story, Mr. Pitt.

TED: Men don't mean to be monsters, but we get caught. We don't intend to go charging into the fray like wild grunting animals!

NORA: Did you say, "caught"?

TED: "The vorpal blade went snicker-snack! He left it dead, and with its head, he went galumphing back."

        CLAIRE knocks quietly on the door.

TED: Yes?

CLAIRE: *(Enters.)* Everything alright then?

TED: We should never have had a child, Claire.

CLAIRE: Ted, Emmett is just fine at boarding school, there was that tough patch, but he's through that now, … what are you saying?

TED: What I'm saying is, *(Begins to unpack.)* I can't even go. Because there is nowhere to go! I am a modern man! *(Starts to exit, then turns back.)* Claire?

CLAIRE: Yes Ted?

TED: Nothing. Nothing. *(He almost says something to NORA, then exits.)*

CLAIRE: *(Looks at NORA.)* The war, you know.

NORA: Me dad died in the war. In the arms of Mr. Tim.

That's why Mr. Tim married me mum. And then went on to kill her. That's what I think, anyway.

CLAIRE: How ghastly. *(Pause.)* Ted's not always like this.

NORA: Oh.

CLAIRE: Lately, he's been worse.

NORA: I see.

CLAIRE: *(Starts to blubber.)* One day, I want to think, this is a perfect day!

NORA: Yes. *(Hands her a tissue.)*

CLAIRE: Everything is how it should be. *(Blows her nose.)*

NORA: That would be nice.

CLAIRE: For just one moment, I want to feel as light as a flock of silver sandpipers on a sunny, windswept beach.

NORA: I often dream that I'm flying up with the birds. When I was young, I actually thought that if I put my mind to it, I could fly with them, And then I thought, bloody hell, I'm going to fly away from this stink hole and save the children of the world from shite. I'm just going to scoop them up and save them. That's what I thought. *(Laughs.)* Anyway Mrs. Pitt, you'll be fine, I know it.

CLAIRE: *(Comic, but sad.)* I just want to have a lively life with love and laughter, that's all I want, that's all I want!!

NORA: Good on you, Mrs. Pitt!

CLAIRE: But serious things keep getting in the way ! Everything just seems so sad, or not right, or disappointing.

ROGER pokes his head in.

ROGER: Oh Claire. *(Spots JANE coming down the hall.)* Oh Jane! *(He enters room and hides behind a plant.)*

                       JANE knocks on the door.

NORA: Come in.

                       CLAIRE hides underneath her scarf.

JANE: *(Pokes her head in.)* Ah. So here you are. Well?

NORA: Well what?

JANE: I'm looking for Marlow. I have some professional business dealings with him. You must know where he is.

NORA: How would I know where anyone is, if I'm just an invisible secret?

JANE: Perhaps some secrets are bigger than other secrets!? *(Pointedly.)* Hello Claire. *(Exits.)*

CLAIRE: What's got into Jane I wonder?

NORA: (Gasps.) Jane was in me dream!

                       ROGER comes out from hiding.

ROGER: That was close.

                       MARLOW knocks on the door. ROGER and CLAIRE hide. NORA opens door. MARLOW pokes his head in.

MARLOW: *(To NORA.)* Ah. There you are.

NORA: Hello Marlow.

MARLOW: Good then. Carry on then. Hello Claire. Hello Roger. *(Exits.)*

ROGER: *(Pops up.)* Hello Marlow. At last, we're alone.

CLAIRE: Not exactly Roger.

ROGER:	Run away with me.
CLAIRE:	What's got into you Roger?
ROGER:	All I know is that this is my house and I can't find a place to lie down with you. What kind of a house is that, I ask you. We have to leave.
CLAIRE:	That's ridiculous Roger.
ROGER:	You mean, you're saying no to me?
CLAIRE:	It's just not a good time.
ROGER:	You are saying no to me!
CLAIRE:	Oh dear. Nora, perhaps we should go make sandwiches for the little female gathering tonight. *(CLAIRE and NORA exit.)*
ROGER:	You're choosing a sandwich over me!? *(Slumps down on bed.)*

TED enters.

TED:	Ah, Roger. Taking my room as well as my wife? Good idea. *(Starts to pack: comic and extreme.)*
ROGER:	My good God, Ted. Let's not be rash. You could just speak your mind, I mean, perhaps you'd feel better. I think I'm up to it, I think I am. We're gentlemen after all.
TED:	Are we Roger? Are we gentlemen? Are you a gentleman?
ROGER:	Look Ted, I didn't mean for it to go this far.
TED:	It's not just you Roger. We're all guilty. I'm just as guilty.
ROGER:	Yes well, it was bound to come out sooner or later and I'd like to extend my...you're guilty? You're guilty too?

TED: Oh yes, I'm guilty too.

ROGER: Oh! Well that comes as a relief. We're both in the same naughty boat, who would have thought, a terrible boat to be in.

TED: And the boat is sinking faster than we can bail.

ROGER: Oh my, quite so. So if you don't mind my asking, who is your guilty paramour? Hah?! Well we know it's not Cousin Daphne. I bet it's the maid, yes you devil you, it's that damn maid, what's her name.

      TED stays intent on packing.

      Well if not the maid, not Daphne, it couldn't be my wife. *(Laughs.)* Don't tell me you're fooling around with my wife! I was beginning to think Jane and Marlow, but not Jane and you! Well?!

TED: This is exactly what I'm talking about.

ROGER: What exactly are you talking about?

TED: As a species, we humans no longer like ourselves. So what do we do? We try to run away from ourselves. We run and we run. Looking for that thing that will make us forget.

ROGER: Forget what ?

TED: That we could destroy ourselves! *(Pulls out a gun.)*

ROGER: I say Ted! You have a gun!

TED: *(Brandishes gun into air.)* We could obliterate the entire human race and everything else while we're at it.

ROGER: Put that thing down Ted!

      They struggle with the gun—comic. They grab it back and forth, interspersed with the following:

TED: It's my gun.

ROGER: Well it's my house. *(Gets the gun.)*

TED: Well that's my gun. *(Gets the gun.)*

ROGER: What about my wife? *(Gets the gun.)*

TED: What about my wife?! *(Gets the gun.)*

ROGER: You're not well!

TED: You like your time and place but I don't. I don't like this century at all.

ROGER: You think I'm a stupid man, don't you? I'm stupid and you're enlightened. Well I'm sorry I never went to war because my feet are flat! But listen here, I'm just struggling like every other fellow. Do you think I like being the president of a company that makes toilets, you can't imagine the jokes, joke, joke, joke., everyone likes a joke.

TED: *(Imitates Groucho Marx.)* "And a heh nonny nonny and a cha cha cha."

ROGER: You're mad!

TED: I'd be less mad if I weren't so damn English.

ROGER: What?

TED: Take this accent.

ROGER: Sorry?!

TED: Why do we talk this way?

ROGER: Because, that's what we do.

TED: We could just stop it.

ROGER: Stop our accent?!

TED: I'm going to stop this twitty, shitty, pip-pip cheerio, I'm going to stop!

ROGER: Don't you dare! *(Lunges at TED. Actors may have to improvise some text. ROGER gets the gun.)* You're not of right mind, I tell you.

TED: *(Speaks with a Canadian accent.)* Not of "right mind"? That's funny, because I've never felt better. Listen. I've stopped being English. I sound, what do I sound like, I sound…Canadian! Yeah. Canadian. Christ almighty! Thanks Roger! *(Exits.)*

ROGER: Stop it! Stop being so mad! And stop sleeping with my wife! Good day. *(Slams the door, realizes where he is, exits and bumps head into JANE.)*

JANE: Ouch! Roger, why must you behave like a rhinoceros?!

ROGER: And why must you behave like an arrogant… eagle.

JANE: Arrogant eagle? *(Sees gun.)* Roger. What are you doing with that gun?

ROGER: What gun? *(He tries to hide it, JANE gets it.)*

JANE: Really, what next?

ROGER: Exactly, what next?!

JANE: Have you seen Marlow? I want to buy one of his inventions. That electric nose warmer of his. For my flight. Across the Atlantic. I'm going to do it Roger.

ROGER: Don't change the subject!

JANE: Did you even hear what I said?!

ROGER: I hate it that you think you're better than me. Well who's on higher moral ground now?

JANE: What are you gabbling about?

ROGER: Who's "gabbling"? Certainly Ted is gabbling, he's even dropped his accent, seems like your affair has unhinged him.

JANE: Who has unhinged who?! Whom? Oh! I don't have time for it. I have things to do.

ROGER: So you're denying your affair with Mr. Straight Jacket.

JANE: More like you're denying your affair with Mrs. Peach.

ROGER: Whoever she is. Look, Miss Eagle. You are my wife and I forbid you to have an affair and I forbid you to fly the Atlantic!

JANE: I will do what I want to do. And fly where I want to fly!

ROGER: Don't listen to me then. I'm just your husband.

JANE: Are you really Roger?

            ROGER runs off and bumps into NORA who is reading a book and carrying several cucumbers. They go flying.

ROGER: Just what kind of a maid are you? What kind, I ask you?!?

NORA: A secret one!

ROGER: What? Oh never mind. Never mind! *(He storms off, bumping into things along the way.)*

NORA: Mrs. Ashbury, if you could disregard that it's me, your old friend who's leaving forever who's talking, last night, I had this dream that *(Sees gun, changes tone.)* Janey, you have a gun.

JANE: It's not my gun, it's Roger's gun.

NORA: Well, what are you going to do with it?

JANE: I don't know, what should we do with it?

NORA: I could lock it up.

JANE: That's best. *(Gives gun to NORA.)*

NORA: Remember old Mr. Hobbs.

TOGETHER: "Keep away from me plums you dirty thieves!"!

> *They laugh, miming what happened. They realize they're being nice to each other and abruptly stop.*

NORA: Anyway Jane! I had a really important dream about you and the Haida chief and…

JANE: *(Interrupts.)* Nora! I have things to do!

NORA: Alright then!

JANE: Alright then!

> *TED enters with a suitcase.*

TED: Jane. How lucky to find you.

JANE: Ted! Where are you going?

TED: *(Newfoundland accent.)* I'm just going. Maybe to Newfoundland. Burt was from Newfoundland. New Found Land.

JANE: You sound strange Ted. Oh Ted! I'm so confused. If I fly across the Atlantic, what if something happened, things do happen.

TED: Follow your heart, Janey McCleod.

JANE: You all need me and don't know that you need me. Who will take charge?!

TED: Oh frabjous day. Calloo Callay! Charge!!

JANE: I don't understand what anyone's talking about anymore.

TED: Exactly.

> *ROGER enters, they dance around each other. TED exits singing "I's the B'y."*

ROGER: Ah hah!

JANE: Oh ah hah nothing. Looking for Claire?

ROGER: Who?

> *DAPHNE enters.*

DAPHNE: Ah! has anyone seen Nora, the maid who's not a maid?

ROGER: Don't talk to me about the damn maid!!

DAPHNE: It was just a simple question.

> *ROGER and DAPHNE exit while MARLOW wheels in his machine that looks like some kind of bad science-fiction thing with a lot of wires. Everyone gets tangled up in it. DAPHNE and ROGER finally manage to exit.*

JANE: Marlow! What on earth is it?

MARLOW: What does it look like? It's a machine, one of my inventions, for Nora and me.

JANE: But what is it?

MARLOW: Going deaf Jane?

JANE: No need to get nasty! I've been looking for you. I was actually going to buy one of your little... gadget things.

MARLOW: They're not gadgets!

JANE: I didn't mean anything by it. Why does everyone misunderstand me!?

> *ROGER enters, fleeing CLAIRE. CLAIRE enters, fleeing TED who is doing a jig.*

CLAIRE: *(Grabs ROGER and whispers.)* Oh Roger, Ted has gone mad. Help me!

ROGER: *(Gesturing frantically to JANE and whispers.)* Not now Peach. We have been suspected.

CLAIRE: Oh mon dieu! *(Exits.)*

JANE: I for one have better things to do than to stand around watching idiocy. And everyone has to stop feeding that bird!

TED: *(To JANE.)* It's a long way to tip a canary, it's a long way to go. It's a long way to tip a Rary, *(Sings.)* to the sweetest gal I know! Exit, stage left. *(Exits after CLAIRE.)*

ROGER: Obviously a code. I will not be cuckolded in my own house I tell you!

MARLOW: You mean, Ted and Jane?! Is something happening between Ted and Jane?!

> *Unnoticed by MARLOW and ROGER, NORA enters with the gun and a padlock. She puts the gun in the bird cage and locks it.*

ROGER: Yes. Maybe. I don't know! Oh confound it all, sometimes I wish I were a hermit. Living in a cave on some island. Just me and…some animals.

MARLOW: There we have it. Why none of us should get married.

ROGER: Hmm.

MARLOW: Why I'm always breaking off my engagements. It's all too bloody difficult, I tell you! How will I ever get married? My eyes are always wandering, they just won't stop. Damn my eyes!

ROGER: You could get married and just play around a bit.

MARLOW: I'm too moral for that. I can't even play around when I'm engaged.

ROGER: Oh. Well you obviously like to play around with maids.

              NORA hides behind the curtain so she can eavesdrop.

MARLOW: What? Ah. Yes. Well that's just "good clean fun," nothing serious. Damn! I should have married Jane after all!

ROGER: Jane?

MARLOW: I mean, uh, this woman. This other woman named Jane. Her name is Jane. Not related to your Jane. She's another Jane.

ROGER: What other Jane?

              CLAIRE enters and hides behind the curtain.

              TED enters doing a jig; he finds NORA, dances with her, exits.

CLAIRE: Oh Roger, Ted is truly insane! Take me away, now!

ROGER: *(Whispers.)* Claire, you must be more discreet. Marlow. *(To room.)* Well now. That's...wonderful. *(To CLAIRE.)* But we can't just go like that. And what about Jane? You know.

              Offstage, the phone rings. JANE answers the phone.

JANE: *(Offstage.)* What!? *(Continues a muffled, anxious conversation.)*

ROGER: What's troubling poor Jane do you suppose?

CLAIRE: It seems to me that you care an awful lot about Jane, all of a sudden.

ROGER: Well, she is my wife after all.

CLAIRE: But you don't have to care that much.

ROGER: Good heavens Claire. *(Laughs.)* Aren't you funny today.

CLAIRE: I can't continue any longer. *(Storms out.)*

ROGER: Well. What do you suppose got into her?

MARLOW: Beats me.

ROGER: *(Feeds the bird.)* Marlow. You and Jane, my Jane, you've been friends and only friends since you were friends, is that correct?

MARLOW: Something like that.

ROGER: Say. That silly bird has the gun.

              CLAIRE enters, and then exits, distraught. NORA steps out of the shadows and is seen by ROGER and MARLOW.

NORA: *(Caught.)* Uh. She's a lot to do to prepare for the séance, as do I, so *(Waves goodbye and starts to exit.)*

ROGER: Séance! There's going to be a séance? In my house?

              TED enters, doing a jig to music. The others start to do the jig. JANE enters.

JANE: Alright. Jig is up! Roger, you did it didn't you?!

ROGER: Did what for heaven's sake?

JANE: You stole my lucky propeller! I can't fly without it; you stole it!

ROGER: I didn't even know you had a lucky propeller!

JANE: It's the one my uncle used in the war and he said it was lucky and he gave it to me!

              JANE points to MARLOW, then NORA. They're taken aback. CLAIRE enters.

CLAIRE: *(To ROGER.)* Have any of you seen Daphne? I want us to leave on the next train.

JANE: Ah-hah! Claire! It was you! You stole my lucky propeller so I would crash!

CLAIRE: Jane! What a wicked thing to say!

JANE: None of you understand. I can't breathe if I don't fly! To fly is to be free of everything. Time stops and you ride through the sky like a lovely, lone planet. A humble passenger on the tail of a whispering wind. I become a wing-ed thing. Safe and sound and alone and away. *(MARLOW yawns.)* I am a pilot, which means that I fly planes. In a plane, with a propeller! I don't know which of you hates me that much, but the latest weather report says that if I'm going to go, I have to go in three days, so I want the thief to return my lucky propeller ! *(Storms out.)*

ROGER: I didn't even know that my wife is superstitious. Why am I the last to know anything around here.

TED: *(Canadian accent.)* But no one knows anything anymore, Roger. We're in a whole new story that has yet to be written.

CLAIRE: That's it. *(To TED and ROGER.)* I will not take any of this any longer. *(Exits.)*

> *TED sings* 'Farewell to Nova Scotia'. *Exits, looking for CLAIRE.*

ROGER: *(Shaky.)* Yesterday, everything seemed fine and normal and how it should be. Now I'm beginning to suspect that it's all falling apart. *(Attempts to tear the padlock off the birdcage.)* I need peace. *(Exits.)*

> *Music. MARLOW and NORA are left alone. NORA stares into space. MARLOW watches her.*

End of Act I.

Act II

Lights up on to MARLOW and NORA, where we last left them. CLAIRE, TED, JANE, ROGER and DAPHNE exit in and out, trying to find each other, trying to escape each other: somewhat surreal. Maybe the set starts to come apart, a door comes off its hinges, or someone gets tangled in curtains and pulls them down, etc.

MARLOW: We seem to live in a mad world.

NORA: I have always thought so.

MARLOW: In some ways life used to be madder.

NORA: Yes.

MARLOW: Yes.

NORA: I suppose so anyway.

MARLOW: But maybe not.

NORA: Exactly. Maybe not. *(She looks for her brooch.)* You haven't seen the brooch, have you? It was the only real present anyone ever gave me. I don't know why you gave it to me, when I'm just a bit of "good clean fun," but anyway, it's lost and I canny like it.

MARLOW: "Good clean fun." Bloody hell, you heard all that stupid drivel come out of my stupid drivel mouth! Drivel, drivel, bloody hell drivel!

NORA: It's alright Marlow.

MARLOW: I didn't mean to say it that way, goddamnit! You're an amazing, you're such a special, you're...

NORA: It really is alright, Marlow.

MARLOW: Stupid, stupid, bloody hell, stupid!

NORA: Marlow, I'm not in love with you.

MARLOW: I'm such a first class idiot!

NORA: Marlow! I'm not in love with you. It's not you that's got me down.

MARLOW: You're not, it isn't? Oh.

NORA: Everyone seems so wounded and confused and... frantic. And Mr. Pitt got me thinking. What if there is another war? I don't think we could stand it. I don't think I could stand it.

MARLOW: I promise you Nora, therre won't be another war.

NORA: And Lady Crunchwell says we'll never sleep again. Really Marlow, think of it. No sleeping. No dreaming. When was the last time you had a good night's sleep!

MARLOW: Maybe we need to learn to dream while our eyes are wide open.

NORA: Sorry?

MARLOW: (Presents his machine.) A gift, Miss Duckworth, from me to you.

NORA: (Gasps.) It's fantastic! How does it work?

MARLOW: To be simple about it, you enter a dream you once had. You can visit that Chief fellow and that raven, for example, whenever you want, Nora. We can even be in each other's dreams at the same time. It's about stimulating parts of the brain, it's very complicated.

NORA: It must signal to the hypothalamus that you're sleeping when in fact you're remembering. Unless it sends a message to the temporal lobe, and it simulates a dream experience, that's also possible.

MARLOW: And how did you get to knowing that?

NORA: I once shared a barn with some cattle and many medical texts.

MARLOW: You're an amazing woman you know that?

NORA: But then I found these other books about the Haida people in Canada. They think our bodies get sick if our souls don't get what they need. But they know every single plant in the forest, Marlow, and they know which ones will make you well again, it's bloody fantastic.

MARLOW: I wish I could ignore the fact that you have beautiful skin. I wish I could ignora Eleanora. Why can't I ignore that?! *(Plunges his head into NORA's neck.)*

NORA: *(Pushes him away.)* Marlow, you're about to get married.

MARLOW: Am I?! Just because I'm engaged, does it mean I'm getting married? Is it a goddamn absolute or something?

NORA: Maybe you should get married Marlow, maybe this time you should just do it.

MARLOW: Why ?!

NORA: I don't know, but maybe you know.

MARLOW: No I don't! So I'm just going to forget about it and I'll just try out this stupid invention, that probably isn't going to work, none of them do, *(Connects them to the machine.)* bloody Jane is bloody right, I'm just one big stupid failure *(Machine begins to hum.)* so sit back and relax because as usual, nothing is going to happen!

> *The machine shoots off sparks. They dream that they are in NORA's flying dream.*

What's happening?!

NORA: We're flying Marlow!

MARLOW: Look at that. *(Laughs.)* My machine works!

NORA: Marlow! Your machine works! *(Laughs.)* We're in my flying dream!

MARLOW: It works! Ah hah! It works! We're flying!

NORA: Goodbye forever Mr. Tim! Whoo!

> *They continue to fly and laugh and have a great time.*

MARLOW: What's that house down there Nora?

NORA: This is your dream now Marlow. You're with someone. I cannit make out who it is.

MARLOW: Bloody hell, it's Jane. Why can't I bloody get rid of that woman?

> *Sparks start to fly and MARLOW gets electrocuted. NORA knows exactly what to do. Comic but impressive.*

You saved my life.

NORA: I did, didn't I?

> *JANE enters.*

JANE: Nora. I need to talk to…oh! *(She's embarrassed to find them so close. She exits and then re-enters.)* Are you alright, Marlow?

MARLOW: I'm alright.

JANE: Alright then. Good then. *(Beat. Exits.)*

NORA: Marlow, you and Jane, I mean, well, maybe you can't get rid of her for a good reason.

MARLOW: Oh.

DAPHNE enters.

DAPHNE: What on earth are you doing dear?

MARLOW: We were flying in my dream machine and then she saved my life.

DAPHNE: Very nice, but now it's my turn. *(Shoos MARLOW away.)*

MARLOW: If only my father could have been here. If only Jane. Thank you Nora. *(Suppresses tears and exits.)*

DAPHNE: Why do the independently wealthy always waste time? Don't waste time Nora Duckworth. Time is precious!

Music. TED enters, dancing like Martha Graham, and then exits.

They're mad as hatters, the lot of them! Nora, I need you to write a very long letter. *(She takes out a letter and a photo from an envelope.)*

NORA: *(Looks at photo.)* What an interesting tree.

DAPHNE: Tree?!

NORA: It could be related to our native willow. Do the leaves have medicinal properties?

DAPHNE: Yes, yes, the tree, but what do we have here? *(Points emphatically.)*

NORA: Where?

DAPHNE: Right there. *(Points to the photo and then to herself, etc.)*

NORA: Lady Crunchwell, it's you! What a beautiful young woman you were. And what a handsome man.

DAPHNE: Yes! Rupert was handsome wasn't he? He was very wealthy, and very handsome. We met in Calcutta in 1862 in a monsoon. We fell head over heels, got engaged, and had a blissful three years together. We were in love Nora. Oh! We were in love.

NORA: And then...

DAPHNE: And then, Rupert changed everything and found God!

NORA: Oh!

DAPHNE: Well Nora, he wanted us to give away all our money and move back to England and live the simple life in a little house with lots of books, a teapot and a bed! Well, I assure you I had no problem with the bed. *(Winks at NORA and laughs.)* But Nora, I was a confirmed atheist and most certainly a rampant materialist, so the idea of living in a little house with God, no linen, and no parties! I would have none of it! I was so angry with him, I wouldn't budge. I was "caught" Nora. I can spot it a mile away. *(Glares at NORA.)*

> *JANE charges through the room wearing goggles and carrying many tools.*

NORA: Crikey bloody hell! What does it take to have a private conversation around here?!

> *TED makes a cross, playing a jazz tune on a harmonica. He looks like Bob Dylan. NORA follows him.*

DAPHNE: Nora! For crying out loud! Just ignore him.

NORA: Sorry, Lady Crunchwell.

DAPHNE: So! Rupert went back to England without me.

He wrote letter after letter and finally got tired of waiting, so he married another woman. I heard that she was exceedingly dull and I heard she died last spring. A few days ago, I received this letter, I didn't dare open it until last night, I just couldn't. Nora, read the letter!

NORA: (Reads.) "My dearest Daphne. How many times I've thought about you, about our love for each other, about our passion that consumed us and then ended so sadly. How I would love to know everything about you. Beautiful Daphy, my stubborn, lovely Daph, please write to me. Obstinately yours, Rupert." It's beautiful, Lady Crunchwell.

DAPHNE: I've wasted my whole life! Humbug? (NORA declines. DAPHNE takes one.) Nora, I need you to be my scribe! But what should I say? And please call me Daphne.

NORA: Daphne. I don't know what you should say, but I know what you should do.

               DAPHNE chokes on her humbug. NORA knows what to do and saves her.

DAPHNE: You saved my life, dear.

NORA: I simply dislodged the humbug from your windpipe. It's an abdominal thrust that I quickly invented when the fruit vendor choked on a grape.

DAPHNE: (Gasps.) Nora Duckworth. There's a modern woman in you just waiting to burst forth. How exciting!

               Beat as NORA takes in this thought. ROGER runs in, pulling CLAIRE with him.

CLAIRE: Daphne!

ROGER: Damn! Why can't we find one empty room!

CLAIRE: I've been looking all over for you. We have a train
             to catch, we have to leave immediately!

DAPHNE: What!

NORA: Oh no Mrs. Pitt. We must have our secret female
             gathering, I made so many sandwiches..

DAPHNE: And your mother dear. She might be expecting us.

CLAIRE: Oh yes! Mother. The sandwiches.

ROGER: But I thought your mother was dead.

CLAIRE: Roger!

ROGER: If you would excuse us. We have to...look for...
             your cushion Daphne.

CLAIRE: She already found her cushion, Roger!

ROGER: (Tries to guide CLAIRE into a closet. Whispers.) We
             have to talk.

CLAIRE: Not in there! I suffer from claustrophobia. I
             shouldn't even be in a house. I should really live
             outside!

ROGER: But we can't talk outside, we can't talk in the house,
             we need, we very much need to be in a cupboard.
             (Physical business as they try to get in.)

             NORA whispers something in DAPHNE's ear.

DAPHNE: I couldn't Nora! (More whispers.) Yes I could! You're
             brilliant, Nora!

CLAIRE: It simply will not work, I won't fit!

NORA: There's a train at midnight, Daphne.

DAPHNE: We'll ring the station, oh Nora! (They exit, whispering
             about their plans.)

ROGER: You could try a bit harder Claire! (Gets a duster in *the eye.)* Ow! Oh for… *(They remain stuck, half way in, half way out. Realizes they're alone.)* Claire. We're alone. We can talk.

CLAIRE: But can we move?

ROGER: Claire, my peach, you have quite misunderstood my concern for my wife being something that it's not. It's just…concern.

CLAIRE: What are we Roger, what are we?

ROGER: What do you mean what are we?

CLAIRE: I want to be free Roger! I want to seek a higher truth. Or just have lovely times. I just want to have lovely times.

ROGER: What are you talking about Claire?! Claire be clear!

JANE appears wearing her goggles and scarf. She watches them.

CLAIRE: Is it making us happy being squished in this box together?

ROGER: Yes, yes, I love being squished in this box with you. I love this.

CLAIRE: Is that what this means Roger? That we love each other? Then we should run away!

ROGER: Yes, yes, yes, oh yes, yes yes.

CLAIRE: Where should we go, where should we go?

ROGER: We could go, we could go, shhh! Somebody's coming.

CLAIRE: I don't hear a thing.

ROGER: We can't be found like this Claire. I want you to be my secret, my once in awhile secret. Ouch!

CLAIRE: Secret! Let me out, it's over! I have to go find the women for our female gathering! *(Manages to escape, exits.)*

ROGER: Claire! I know I'm weak! I've always been weak, I have no willpower but goddamn it! That makes me strong! I know what I want. Claire! *(Sees JANE.)* Jane!

JANE: *(Looks at mop.)* Are you our new maid?

ROGER: Jane, I can explain.

JANE: Roger. Listen. Nora the maid is my childhood friend, my best friend, or she used to be my best friend, and I grew up a poor parson's daughter and I married you for your money!

ROGER: Is that really true Jane?

JANE: Um. Which part?

ROGER: Parson's daughter, alright. Nora's friend, explains a lot. But marrying me for my money?

JANE: Something like that.

ROGER: I see. And what about Ted? What about Marlow? You think I'm quite stupid don't you!

JANE: I won't answer that Roger. I've got to run. *(Exits.)*

ROGER: Jane! Claire! *(Exits and bumps into TED.)* Ted! *(They do a dance of getting out of the way.)* Ahh! Just get out of my way! I have to find Claire. No. I have to find my wife. My wife. Yes.

TED: *(Smoking a Groucho cigar.)* I'm looking for my wife as well, why don't we look together?

ROGER: No ! I want to find her myself. Now, just go away! *(Flings TED across the room a la Marx Brothers. A loud crash.)*

TED: (*Re-enters. Speaks with an English accent.*) "An iron had entered his soul which bereft him of pride and of realm!"E.J. Pratt. Great Canadian poet.

ROGER: What is it with you and Canada?! (*Exits, re-enters.*) Say. Your accent's back. Well that's one thing. (*Exits.*)

TED: "He was old, yet it was not his age which made him roost on the crags like a rain-drenched raven." Damn. I'm bloody English again.

> *CLAIRE enters and crosses in from of TED. Stops. They look at each other. Sad beat. She exits. MARLOW enters and taps TED on the shoulder. They scream back and forth.*

MARLOW: Ted! Let's stop screaming like women shall we?

> *JANE enters. MARLOW and TED scream.*

Well, well, well. Are you still here?

JANE: Hello Ted.

TED: Hello Jane. (*Tries again.*) Hello Jane.

JANE: Hello Ted.

TED: Hello Jane. Damn it.

MARLOW: No greeting for me Jane?

JANE: Ah Marlow! Are you here too? Anyway, you should both know that I've decided to throw caution to the wind and fly across the Atlantic with another propeller.

MARLOW: Ah. You're sure it's wise to disregard the power of a good luck charm?

JANE: No. I mean yes! Pashaw! Good luck charm. Who needs one? Not me. Pashaw! If you'll excuse me I have an engagement.

TED: *(English accent.)* I'm going to miss you something fierce, Jane. I wish I could say without sounding English, don't go! In fact, that's what I will say. Damn it Jane. Don't go. *(Scottish accent.)* Damn it Jane, don't go. *(Irish accent.)* Don't go Jane, don't go. *(Another English accent.)* It's no use, who am I kidding.

> *JANE stares at him bewilderedly. ROGER enters.*

ROGER: Ah hah! With both of them at the same time no less.

JANE: Oh dear, I've been found out.

ROGER: We'll see who has the last laugh. Oh yes. We will see. *(Grabs bird cage and exits.)*

JANE: Look. I have to dash.

MARLOW: As do we. *(Holds back TED.)* You don't perhaps have any inside information as to when the women are having their little séance?

TED: A séance? Oh but Claire wouldn't allow us. Men make the spirits shy.

MARLOW: What a brilliant idea, Ted.

> *MARLOW motions TED to follow him. JANE starts to run the other way and bumps into CLAIRE.*
>
> *CLAIRE is wearing a ridiculous turban and is draped in veils. They scream. They stare at each other. JANE starts to exit.*

CLAIRE: Jane! Oh. Never mind.

JANE: Do you want me to apologize for accusing you of stealing my propeller or do you want to apologize for ruining my marriage?

CLAIRE: Oh Jane, I knew it! You know!

JANE: Well I'm not blind. But why don't we say that we both apologized and then let's pretend we both feel fine.

CLAIRE: Alright.

JANE: Good then.

CLAIRE: And so you'll make it to our female gathering?

JANE: No. Yes. I don't know! But first I have to ring my mechanic. I'm going to do it Claire! Fly across the Atlantic with another propeller, I mean.

CLAIRE: Good for you Jane!!

JANE: Oh, I suppose. Self-doubt, you know.

CLAIRE: No. I don't have that. Just guilt and disappointment.

JANE: Oh. Right then. Off we go then.

CLAIRE: Off we go, Jane!

They exit. Music. Everyone enters and exits. MARLOW enters with a bundle of clothes, exits with TED. JANE makes her phone call and gasps, "What?!" DAPHNE and NORA enter with a suitcase and then make a phone call to the train station. ROGER returns the birdcage that is now missing its door and the gun, then looks for MARLOW and TED. DAPHNE makes a phone call by herself. CLAIRE looks for DAPHNE. NORA brings in large tray of sandwiches, table and chairs. She notices the birdcage. JANE enters, distraught.

JANE: Nora!

NORA drops sandwiches.

Nora! My mechanic just told me that a strange man called him and said "Tell Jane to give up on winning the title. If she tries, she'll die!" Just like that!

NORA: Jane, listen to me! I've been trying to tell you about that dream I had, you were flying across the Atlantic and you were talking to that Haida chief who I thought was my spiritual guide, but now I realize that he is really me, and in me dream, you were talking to him, in other words you were talking to me, and you said

JANE: Nora! Ah don't want to hear about Haida chiefs or spiritual guides or any nonsense about you being him and him being you; ah don't want to bloody hear any of it because, he doesn't exist!

NORA: Aal reet then!

JANE: Aal reet then!

NORA: And I suppose you don't want to hear that the gun is missing.

JANE: It is? *(Puts her fingers in her ears.)* No! I don't even want to hear that.

    CLAIRE enters.

CLAIRE: Ah! Now we just need Daphne!

    DAPHNE enters.

DAPHNE: Boo!

CLAIRE: *(Startled.)* Really Daphne.

DAPHNE: Forgive me for keeping the spectres waiting. Not that they really exist.

CLAIRE: You don't fool me a bit. Ladies. Please be seated. There's a certain charge in the air, can you feel it?

JANE: Well no , not really.

DAPHNE: No, I can't say that I do.

NORA: Sorry Mrs. Pitt, I don't feel anything either.

CLAIRE: *(Interrupts.)* Ladies. Shhhh. *(Lights a candle.*

> *DAPHNE has a sandwich.*

Daphne.

> *NORA has a sandwich.*

Nora!

> *They finally hold hands.*

Concentrate on the flame of life. Feel the energy in the room. Those who have lived and died before us are here with us. Feel their presence. Breathe them in and breathe them out. Breathe them in and breathe them out.

DAPHNE: I hope it's alright that I just pretend to breathe.

CLAIRE: Shh.

DAPHNE: That turban quite becomes you Clarabelle.

CLAIRE: Daphne. Shhh.

DAPHNE: It reminds me of our trip to Paris in 1925. You were wearing my scarf from India on your head.

CLAIRE: Daphne! Be quiet! Silence won't kill you!

DAPHNE: Yes it will dear, but that's alright, I just wanted to say that was a very good trip.

JANE: I'm not even sure why I'm here. I don't have time to talk to a group of ghosts.

CLAIRE: Spirits Jane ! Not ghosts. please!

JANE: I didn't know there was a difference.

NORA: *(Incredulous.)* Jane!

JANE: Well I didn't.

CLAIRE: Ladies! Concentrate. We have gathered here to ask the spirits, our dead loved ones, the ones who moved on, who are not trapped like ghosts, to ask them about our lives. How do we reconnect with our lives. How do we feel alive in our lives. Truly alive. Not dead. But alive.

DAPHNE: A bit much Claire.

                CLAIRE takes off her turban, as if she's giving up.

                Sorry dear. You're doing wonderfully.

NORA: Please keep going Mrs. Pitt.

DAPHNE: Yes, Nora needs to find out whether Mr. Tim murdered her poor mother.

NORA: What I really want to ask is about me future.

DAPHNE: And you might want to ask about that Roger fellow as well.

CLAIRE: Oh yes. Mr. Tim, the future, Roger, oh dear, what about Roger? What about Ted?! What about me?!

                CLAIRE has an emotional collapse on the table. Pause.

JANE: *(Whispers.)* Claire , um, I guess I could ask if...you know.

CLAIRE: Know what Jane?

JANE: You know. Whether I should *("Mimes" flying over the Atlantic. CLAIRE still doesn't understand.)* Fly across the Atlantic, for God's sake. Should I fly across the Atlantic?!

NORA: Bloody hell, Jane, if you'd only let me.

JANE: *(Interrupts.)* Should I go? That's all I want to know. And who doesn't want me to go? There's a man who doesn't want me to go. Who is he?

NORA: I as well, have a question about me own life.

JANE: Not about Marlow, I hope.

NORA: No Jane! It's not about Marlow.

CLAIRE: Ladies. Calmez-vous s'il vous plait! I will try to contact mother. *(Wipes away a tear.)* Maman! It's 1936, we want to talk to you. Are you here? *(Three knocks. The women gasp.)* Maman, should Jane Ashbury née McCleod, fly across the gigantic Atlantic? Should she attempt to win the title? Maman. Talk to us. If Jane should go, knock two times, if she shouldn't go, knock three times!

Two knocks. JANE gasps. And then there is a third knock.

DAPHNE: Well that's just confusing.

Comical improvised banter as the women discuss whether CLAIRE had said threes for 'go', or three knocks for 'don't go'. The curtains blow. Scary music. A door slams. The women scream. Footsteps echo. TED and MARLOW appear out of the shadows dressed as frumpy women. The women scream.

TED/
MARLOW: Room for two more?

CLAIRE: You scared us half to death!

JANE: Was it you two who made that knocking?

MARLOW: What knocking?

ROGER enters.

ROGER: Ah hah!

He attacks MARLOW kind of limply. Everyone is somewhat confused. He then attacks TED, and then ROGER takes out the gun. Everyone gasps.

Oh never mind.

MARLOW: What was that all about?

ROGER: I don't know. Somehow I can't be bothered. I have an unfaithful wife and a gun but somehow I just can't be bothered. *(ROGER puts the gun on the table.)*

CLAIRE: Give me strength. *(Pushes the gun aside.)* What are the men doing at our séance!

JANE: *(Whispers.)* Claire, just let them stay. We were just beginning to get somewhere.

CLAIRE: Fine. But you men must take this seriously or I'll have you dismissed.

> *The men mumble solemn promises that they'll be good, etc. They find chairs and sit down. MARLOW sits on NORA's brooch and screams.*

NORA: My brooch! *(Beat.)* Thanks Marlow. *(Sits.)*

MARLOW: Don't mention it. *(Rubs his bum.)* Ow.

DAPHNE: *(To CLAIRE.)* Try to speed things up a bit dear.

CLAIRE: Shh! Come back to us Mother. Are you still with us? Come back to us Maman!

TED: *(Has a vision. Spooky music.)* "I've chased the shouting wind along and flung my eager craft through footless halls of air, up, up the long, delirious burning blue, I've topped the wind-swept heights with easy grace where never lark, or even eagle flew." By John Gillespie Magee. Killed in action in 1940 when he was just nineteen.

EVERONE: *(Gently.)* Ted!

NORA: It's beautiful.

JANE: *(In awe.)* It's 1936, Ted. 1940 isn't here yet!

TED: The whole of the 20th century is jammed in my

head. There's a very big cloud shaped like a mushroom and skin melting off bones, and the people in tthe Empire, mad as hell and won't take it anymore! The corruption, the Cars! The traffic jams! The world is a precarious, and very anxious mess, and it's getting worse by the second.

CLAIRE: Oh Ted.

TED: We do everything for oil. It all boils down to oil.

CLAIRE: Ted.

TED: We'll have the technology to save ourselves, and we won't use it, it's astounding!

CLAIRE: Ted.

TED: We're careening out of control on a road to complete annihilation…

CLAIRE: Ted!

TED: …and we won't admit it. We're in such a deep state of denial that we can't even admit there's a gun on the table. In fact! We can't even admit that this bird is dead.

EVERYONE: Ted!

TED: *(Becomes John Cleese in Monty Python's 'Dead Parrot Sketch.')* It's not breathing. It has passed on. This bird has ceased to be. It is no more! It has gone to meet its maker. *(Yells in its ear.)* Hello Polly!

CLAIRE draws TED to the side of the room.

CLAIRE: Stop it Ted! Stop it! It hurts too much!

JANE: It's just a bit stunned.

NORA: Yeah. It's resting. *(Pokes the bird.)*

TED: I'm sorry I got sick Claire, I'm sorry I got sick.

CLAIRE: Not now Ted. Not now. *(Poignant beat.)*

ROGER: *(Whispers.)* Claire! Claire!

JANE: Roger!

CLAIRE: *(Returns to table.)* Ladies, where were we?

               Improvised banter.

JANE: I know! We were just about to find out if your
               mother said I should go, or should not go.

               They inhale and exhale. Spooky music.

MARLOW: IjustrememberedadreamIhad.*(Feignsremembering.)*
               Jane, it's about you. It was... Oh God. Oh no.

JANE: Marlow?! What was the dream?

MARLOW: A crash. Never mind.. It was just a dream. *(Flinches.)*
               Oh God.

NORA: I guess my dream doesn't count.

JANE: Keep breathing Marlow. Let the spirits know that
               you're here.

MARLOW: Is this just a vision or what is it. Why is Jane crashing
               in this dream?

ROGER: *(Whispers.)* Claire...

TED: I keep seeing visions of the downward spiral into
               chaos.

ROGER: I don't seem to be getting any visions at all.

JANE: Why doesn't that surprise me? !

ROGER: You're not the only one who wants answers. I
               would also love it if a wayward spirit told me what
               to do and what not to do. I would really love that.

JANE: You don't need a spirit to tell you a thing or two.

ROGER: Have something to get off your chest Jane?

JANE: Yes Roger. Perhaps it would interest a few people present, that your little affair with Claire, isn't your first.

CLAIRE: Roger!

ROGER: Don't you want to tell the table about your affairs?

JANE: I haven't had any!

CLAIRE: Oh Roger. *(Collapses on table.)*

ROGER: Look, all I really wanted was to roll around with Claire in some secret room and squeeze her beautiful peaches. *(Everyone gasps.)* What's wrong with that ? It's a bloody good escape from being a president of a bloody toilet company.

DAPHNE: If the spirits haven't run away in horror, they're better people than I.

ROGER: An escape from the fact that everyone thinks you're stupid and no one loves you, not even your wife!

JANE: Well don't expect an apology from me.

NORA: No one would ever get an apology from Jane!

JANE: Now what?

NORA: You never, ever apologize. I don't think you ever have, not once. You just tell me what to do, what to think, what not to think. Well, I'm tired of doing this, or not doing that, dreaming this, but not dreaming that for you or Mr. Tim or anyone. I'm tired of people thinking I'm a wee daft thing.

JANE: Oh Nora.

DAPHNE: Ah! So that's what it is! Nora is being held hostage by the emotional pain of a traumatic past. It's the past.

EVERYONE: *(Beat.)* Well you could say the same about me too. *(Improvised banter.)*

DAPHNE: But Nora reminds me of a bird with a broken wing. There's nothing more beautifully tragic than a bird with a broken wing.

EVERYONE: Oh.

CLAIRE: Maman!

> *They all scream and jump away from the haunted chair.*

ROGER: Get away from the chair, Claire!

MARLOW: Look! *(He runs to the window and "finds" a note stuck to it. Letters are pasted to it like a ransom note.)* Oh Jane. Doesn't look good. *(Hands it to her.)*

JANE: *(Reads.)* "Jane. Do not go. Beware of the Atlantic!" *(Everyone gasps.)* Wait a minute. A ghost didn't do this. A ghost can't use glue.

NORA: *(Whispers.)* Daphne. Look at the time. The train. You have to go!

> *DAPHNE gasps loudly.*

CLAIRE: What is it Daphne?!

DAPHNE: I'm sure it was nothing but I thought I saw two men lurking in the garden.

> *CLAIRE looks alarmed, NORA looks at her quizzically. DAPHNE gasps.*

CLAIRE: For heaven's sake Daphne, why do you keep gasping? !

DAPHNE: I can't quite be sure, but I'm sure I saw two suspicious looking men, they're carrying a sack, a sack large enough to put say, someone my size into.

CLAIRE:	I don't see anyone out there, you're scaring me half to death.
JANE:	*(Holds on to the back of CLAIRE's chair. It starts to vibrate. Everyone gasps. She notices MARLOW's gadget on CLAIRE's chair.)* Marlow… Isn't this your gadget?
EVERYONE:	Marlow!
JANE:	*(Takes some glue out MARLOW's pocket.)* And what do we have here? Glue.
EVERYONE:	Marlow!
MARLOW:	It wasn't me.
EVERYONE:	Marlow!
MARLOW:	Alright! I confess! It was I. I did it, I stole your propeller.
EVERYONE:	Marlow!
MARLOW:	And I phoned your mechanic, and I made the spooky knocks with my spooky knock machine, and the vibrating chair, and the note.
EVERYONE:	Why?
MARLOW:	Because goddamn it! I'm sick of feeling like a failure. And I'm sick of you making digs about my inventions and my father not being proud. Wouldn't I love to wear a scarf that flaps in the wind too, goddamn it! Wouldn't I just love one little moment of glory, one little moment of "well done, Marlow Stokes, well done!" Wouldn't I just love that. *(Overcome with emotion.)*
JANE:	Marlow. If you only knew how sad and lost I've always been!
NORA:	Sad and lost?

JANE: And lonely too.

ROGER: Lonely too?

JANE: I thought it was so obvious!

TED/
DAPHNE: Obvious to me.

MARLOW: Anyway folks, back to me, remember me! We were
             talking about me! I just wanted to say that at first
             it was all that, but then it became something quite
             different. I may be a lost coward, a jealous cheat
             and a hopeless womanizer, but as maddening as I
             find you, the thought of you falling out of the sky
             into the cold, black Atlantic, all alone, is, well…not
             a pleasant thought.

             Boisterous banter of agreement all around.

DAPHNE: *(Yelling over the din.)* For heaven's sake, be quiet!

             They all stop in amazement.

             It's time you did something, my dears! Time is
             precious! Ted! You could start a group, or even write
             a book! Claire, use that excellent brain of yours, my
             darling. Dig deep and find yourself. Marlow, learn
             to really love; your adolescence is getting tedious,
             my dear. Roger, you feel stupid because you are
             stupid, perhaps you should do something about
             that. And Nora and Jane, forgive each other before
             it's too late. All of you, stop being so stuck! Take
             better care of life. Take it from me, one who didn't.
             Please, my dears! *(Looks out to the garden.)*

             *Knocks on the table. Gasps. The lights go out.
             DAPHNE screams. Sounds of scuffling. A gun shot.
             Screams.*

CLAIRE: Roger, turn on the lights, quickly.

ROGER: I can't see a blessed thing.

JANE: Here, here, here' s the light. *(Turns it on. DAPHNE is gone.)*

CLAIRE: Daphne? Where's Daphne? Oh my god. The men in the garden! Daphne!

CLAIRE, ROGER, JANE and NORA run out to the garden.

MARLOW sits beside TED.

MARLOW: I'm not really getting married Ted. I broke it off months ago.

TED: Somehow I knew that.

MARLOW: I have to stop standing still Ted.

TED: In the trenches we didn't stop moving. No, that's not true. Sometimes we didn't move at all. It was hideous. The weight of a dead man and then the lightness of another.

CLAIRE, ROGER, NORA and JANE come running in.

CLAIRE: Oh Ted, Daphne's vanished into thin air!

TED: Try not to panic Claire, perhaps she's in her room.

CLAIRE: Yes ! We must look in her room.

CLAIRE and NORA exit. ROGER and JANE collide.

ROGER: Look Jane. Awfully sorry about everything.

JANE: Oh Roger. I did love you. A little bit. Sort of.

ROGER: Thanks Jane. As I did you. Sort of.

JANE gives him her wedding ring. A warm moment. They run out, JANE smashes into NORA.

JANE: Nora! I'm sorry I've been such a bad friend and

kept you a secret. And I bet that dream of yours told you what I didn't want to know. That I'm not experienced enough to fly the Atlantic. And guess what? You're right. I will always fly but I'm not going to fly o'er the Atlantic because I don't want to. Nora! Did you hear what I just said? I don't want to do it! I'm not going to fly the Atlantic!

JANE and NORA laugh and embrace. MARLOW and TED applaud.

But now we should save Daphne.

TOGETHER: Daphne! *(They run off and stop to look at the bird.)*

NORA: It's just a bit stunned.

JANE: Yeah. Just a bit stunned.

            They exit.

TED: I *could* start up a group. We veterans could warn people about the evils of the war machine and all that.

MARLOW: Perhaps there's hope.

TED: I do see a few good things in the future.

MARLOW: Glad to hear it Ted.

            A scream from off stage.

TED: Marlow! We have to go help!

MARLOW: My God, we have to go help!

            They exit and collide with CLAIRE, ROGER, NORA and JANE.

CLAIRE: Ted. She's been abducted. There was a note. In her room.

TED: Well, we should ring Scotland Yard.

CLAIRE: Oh yes Ted! Scotland Yard!

Everyone runs around looking for the phone. NORA notices an envelope on the table that is addressed to her and opens it.

CLAIRE: My cousin has been abducted and we can't find the phone. What kind of house is this?!

ROGER: It's a perfectly fine house!

EVERYONE but NORA: Then where's the phone?

ROGER: Probably with the abductors and the abductee, probably the phone was abducted, It makes sense to me.

NORA: The phone wasn't abducted. The phone is right here.

CLAIRE: My God, it's the phone. Call Scotland Yard. *(She leaps on the phone and calls operator.)* Operator! Operator! My cousin, Daphne Crunchwell has been abducted. Yes. We were having a séance and Daphne was giving us a rather long-winded speech and then she saw some suspicious men with sacks in the garden and then there was a gunshot and then she was gone, abducted, in the dark, completely and utterly abducted!

NORA: *(Yells.)* She was not abducted!!

CLAIRE: I'll call you back sir, a little something has come up. *(Hangs up.)* Nora. What do you mean Daphne was not abducted?!

NORA: She was not abducted, she fled.

EVERONE: Fled!

CLAIRE: But why would anyone abduct a 95-year-old woman who has fled?

EVERYONE: She wasn't abducted! She fled!

CLAIRE: Alright.

NORA: She went to the North Country to be with her first and only love, Rupert Noseworthy. They're going to hold each other at long last, I arranged a train ticket so she could go up there this evening, but this letter, I don't believe it!

EVERYONE: What?

NORA: *(Reads.)* "Nora dear. I decided to not waste any more time, so I hired the mechanic's son to fly me up there instead.

JANE: The mechanic's son?

ROGER: Who in God's name is he?

JANE: The mechanic's son.

ROGER: Ah.

NORA: "I paid the cook to turn off the lights when I knocked on the table, then I shot the gun, purely for dramatic effect. and then I snuck out and met the mechanic's son at that field down the way. By the time you read this note I will be getting in Jane's plane."

              The sound of a plane taking off. JANE runs to look.

JANE: No! I don't believe it. The nerve! She stole my plane! She stole my plane!

NORA: "Tell Jane she'll get her beloved plane back early tomorrow morning. " *(Shows JANE the letter, JANE takes it.)*

JANE: Oh.

CLAIRE: Oh Daphne. *(Wipes away tears.)*

JANE: P.S. Nora dear. You know what you are. Now go

be it! P.P.S. Godspeed the wonderful, shoddy lot of you. Obstinately yours, Daphne Crunchwell.

CLAIRE blows her nose.

TED: Claire. If you can stand it that I might go mad from time to time, let's go home my darling.

CLAIRE: Oh Ted! Perhaps one day we'll move to Newfoundland, or India! I could get a degree in theology. Or I could teach yoga to women who have a spiritual hole. There's so much to do.

TED: So much to do. *(They embrace.)*

Everyone cheers.

ROGER: And I, I am going to my study. I have some… studying to do.

Everyone cheers, pats him on the back.

MARLOW: Well Jane. Now that you're not going to fly across the gigantic Atlantic, what are you going to do?

JANE: I thought I'd take a good old boat to Tahiti with a certain someone who invents gadgets.

MARLOW: *(Smiling.)* They're not gadgets.

JANE: Oh be quiet! *(Passionately kisses MARLOW.)*

ROGER: Ah hah! *(Beat. Everyone looks concerned.)* Never mind. Carry on.

Everyone applauds. MARLOW and JANE laugh. They kiss again. NORA looks out the window.

Nora, you know you can stay here as long as you like.

NORA: Thanks Roger, but I have a few things I want to get done. First, I'm going to study about medicinal plants with the Haida on Haida Gwaii, an island in western Canada.

EVERYONE: Oh.

NORA: And then I'll disguise meself as a man and I'll fish
               for halibut; I'll make gobs of money!

EVERYONE: (Impressed.) Gobs of money!

NORA: And then I'll come back to England to work with
               children who've had a tough go of it. After all that
               I'll be ready to study medicine. I'm going to be a
               doctor.

EVERYONE: A doctor! Nora, a doctor! Dr. Duckworth! (They
               applaud and cheer.)

NORA: Wait! Before the world falls into chaos once again,
               I say that Jane takes me flying!

They all cheer. TED puts on Latin music and they dance exuberantly.
               The music changes to something ominous. Sound
               of a bomb falling. They look at the audience, and
               raise their arms as if they're about to fly.

Lights out.

The End.